WHO *Am I*

DISCOVERING THE VALUE AND WORTH OF WOMEN

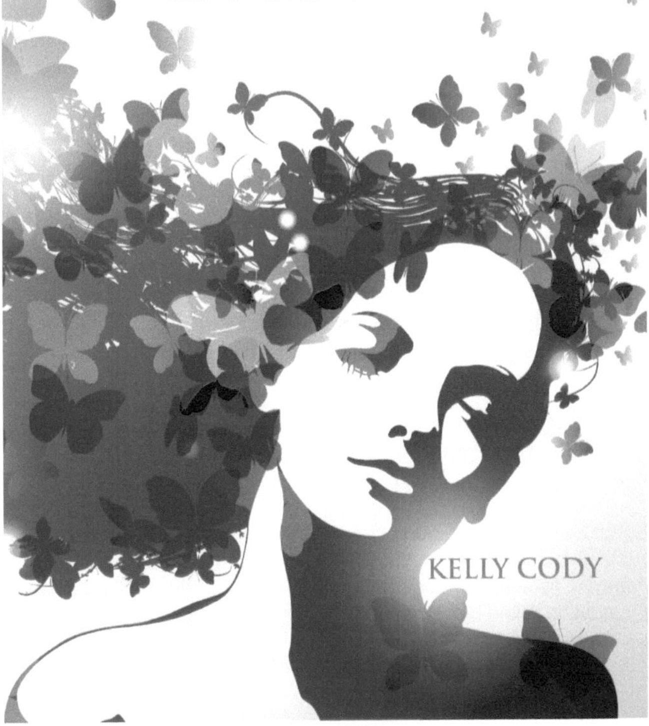

KELLY CODY

xulon PRESS

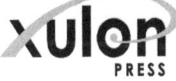

Copyright © 2015 by Kelly Cody

Who Am I
Discovering the Value and Worth of Women
by Kelly Cody

Printed in the United States of America.

Edited by Xulon Press

ISBN 9781498434041

All rights reserved solely by the author. The author guarantees all contents are original and do not infringe upon the legal rights of any other person or work. No part of this publication may be reproduced, stored in a retrieval system or transmitted in any form or by any means – electronic, mechanical, photocopy, recording, or any other – except for brief quotations in printed reviews, without the prior permission of the author. The views expressed in this book are not necessarily those of the publisher.

Scripture quotations taken from the *Holy Bible, New Living Translation*. Copyright ©1996, 2004by Tyndale House Foundation. Used by permission of Tyndale House Publishers, Inc.

Scripture quotations taken from the New King James Version (NKJV). Copyright © 1982 by Thomas Nelson, Inc. Used by permission. All rights reserved.

Scripture quotations taken from *The Message* (MSG). Copyright © 1993, 1994, 1995, 1996, 2000, 2001, 2002. Used by permission of NavPress Publishing Group. Used by permission. All rights reserved.

Scripture quotations taken from *The Amplified Bible* (AMP*)*, *Old Testament.* Copyright © 1965, 1987 by The Zondervan Corporation. *The Amplified New Testament*, copyright 1954, 1958, 1987 by The Lockman Foundation. Used by permission. All rights reserved.

Front cover image designed by blinkblink/Shutterstock.com

www.xulonpress.com

This is my commandment: Love each other in the same way I have loved you. There is no greater love than to lay down one's life for one's friend.
~ John 15:12-13

This book is dedicated to the many women who have been impacted by violence and to my five beautiful children; Raiana, Sierra, Paris, Ja'Shua, and Mariah, you are my greatest gifts from God. I love you.

A portion of the proceeds from this book will be donated toward helping to end violence against women.

CONTENTS

FOREWORD xiii
CHAPTER 1: COMMUNICATION IS KEY 15
CHAPTER 2: THE JOURNEY 19
CHAPTER 3: MARTHA, MARTHA
              DO YOU HEAR ME? 25
CHAPTER 4: MIND OVER MATTER 29
CHAPTER 5: THE POWER IN THE WOMB . . . 39
CHAPTER 6: WHO AM I 47
CHAPTER 7: NOTHING CLOSE
              TO NORMAL 51
CHAPTER 8: TILL' DEATH DO US PART 59
CHAPTER 9: POWER AND CONTROL
              VS. LOVE 67
CHAPTER 10: A NEW JOURNEY,
               A NEW LIFE 79
CONCLUSION. 85
ACKNOWLEDGMENTS. 91
GOD'S PROMISES 93
ENDNOTES 97

FOREWORD

*O*ften times I look back on where I came from to remember how far I have traveled. When people ask me, "How did you do it?" there is nothing more to say but…..God.

Holy Spirit have your way. God, you are amazing and the great creator of everything; I thank you for who you are and how you have transformed me. Heavenly Father, I thank you for impacting the lives of women all around the world to understand their value and worth through the reading of this book. I pray that each set of hands and eyes that are able to read this book are encouraged and develop a clearer understanding of your intentions and plans for them. Thank you my Lord, my Savior, and Heavenly Father for letting us see and experience your love, your mercy, your favor, and your grace through this book. Thank you, God, for using me to type each word for the encouragement and guidance of others. Thank you for creating me worthy.

In Jesus' mighty name I pray, Amen.

Chapter 1

COMMUNICATION IS KEY

One of the most important factors when understanding our value and worth as women is the understanding of what God says about us and how He sees us. This is found through hearing Him and through the interpretation of His Word. The way in which women interpret scriptures contributes to the way we see ourselves and the way we identify our significance. Unfortunately, sometimes the biblical scriptures we relate to as women are merely pointing out wifely submission. These scriptures focus more on wifely obedience than on partnership.

Depending on our interpretation and any teachings we have received of these scriptures, they can emphasize role inferiority and can be leverage for misuse which often times encourages female weakness, reticence, and oppression. God did not create us with these characteristics and any negative thought or feeling we have about ourselves was never His intention for us. Misuse, misunderstanding and misapplication of scripture have led to the devaluing of women, reduced self-esteem and been an increased safety risk for women if in the wrong hands. Biblical literacy with regards to who God says we are can help women to understand their value and worth and encourage and restore their role in the Kingdom of God.

According to the Holy Bible, Jesus expressed his love and value for women during each encounter despite the culture of patriarch-ism that was influenced and imposed by the Greek community. Women were seen as inferior to men. Deprivation of education, seclusion, and slavery were the roles of women. Despite these indifferences, there are many accounts of interactions between women and Jesus. Women who were objectified, shunned, and even seen as unclean and adulterous were ushered into the presence of Jesus. Through the actions of Jesus, it is apparent that He was not concerned about women's roles that were set forth by society; He was more concerned about the relationship with women.

Despite the time and era of women being objectified, Jesus exemplified women's importance. These women were seen as worthless who cried, sinned, and experienced bodily discharge. God did not look down on women, in fact; He praised them for their assertion, passion, and devotion. Throughout the Holy Bible, there are several stories that illustrate Jesus as encouraging women and valuing them as more than a piece of property. During this time; He challenged the societal norms through His actions and valued the contributions women provided, despite what society deemed unworthy and worthless.

> *For although the first woman came from man, every other man was born from woman, and everything comes from God. (1 Corinthians 11:12 NLT)*

This scripture is an important word from the Heavenly Father. In this scripture He clarifies that without women, man would not exist and without man; woman would not have been created. This scripture is crucial to understand because in it we see the importance of relationships. We see how one gender needs the other and how men and women are meant to cohabitate together in the world. Satan's plan and plow was to bring division to man and woman because their original purpose was to enhance the Kingdom of God.

God tells us in His word that *"The thief does not come except to steal, and to kill, and to destroy." (John 10:10 NKJV)* Therefore, if Satan can disrupt the purpose of men and women in any way; he will, and he will stop at nothing to accomplish his mission. This is why we have doubt, confusion, worry, anxiety, and fear, especially in male-female relationships. If Satan can influence the mind of men and women with sin, he knows it will cause such an unworthy feeling that we become immovable, mentally, and we begin to believe and tell our subconscious mind that we are worthless. These thoughts incapacitate us mentally and reduce the probability of us walking in the purpose God has for us.

In most battles and wars one of the objectives to having your opponent, lose, succumb and/or surrender is to negatively impact or cause chaos upon them. In most wars and battles the primary attack is on the communication system. Therefore, we see something in common between the attacks of Satan on our relationship with God and our relationships with others. This is very similar to any other war or battle that has been fought. Satan attacks our communication. With this knowledge we must work to improve and increase our communication with God and in other relationships.

CHAPTER 2

THE JOURNEY

Over the last few years; I have been given the opportunity to study the Word of God to seek an understanding of the importance, worth, and the significance of women. This has been an amazing journey of which I feel extremely blessed to have been given to share. As stated previously; this book is written out of obedience to encourage women to move out of bondage and into what God has planned for their lives since the beginning of creation.

When God gave me this task, I did not really know why except for the fact that I was at a place in my life where I questioned why I was alive, who I am, and what I had to offer. I wasn't quite sure how God could use me. I felt like the most unlikely woman to be used for anything. I asked Him to open my eyes and show me who I am to Him and why I exist. Everything He showed me helped to change my way of thinking and feeling, and my actions began to change based on the change my heart underwent through this process. This journey has healed me of past pains and allowed me to feel and know the love of God. He took me, the most unlikely of people to share His love, His intentions, and a small peek into the creation of women.

God has so much more in store for women; however, He is waiting for us to take a step of faith. That step of faith is to trust in Him and to release past hurts, painful situations, memories and events that hinder us from walking in the purpose and plans He has for us. He wants to make us whole again, but we have to allow Him the opportunity. We as women have to realize what it means to be forgiven, to let go of our sins–forgive ourselves, forgive others, and eradicate the lies Satan has led us to believe for years. God's plan from the moment we were created was for women to be perfect, without a blemish, and for her to impact the world.

Let's start at the beginning when God created us. For years I believed, based on teachings from the church's I had attended that somehow I was accountable for Eve eating of the fruit and giving it to her husband. This thought somehow held me in bondage and at times I found myself doubting my value based merely on the thought of being a failure to mankind. I'm not sure if I was the only one that felt this way, however, this was one of the first lies the Holy Spirit helped me to uncover through His guidance and revelation of the following scriptures.

And the Lord God said, "It is not good that man should be alone; I will make him a helper comparable to him." (Genesis 2:18 NKJV)

According to the Merriam Webster Dictionary online (2015), the word helper is defined as "a person that helps or gives assistance and support" and the word "help" is defined as "to do something that makes it easier for someone to do a job, to deal with a problem, etc: to aid or assist someone" and to make something less severe: to make something more pleasant or easier to deal with." God not only was clear of His intention for us, He was also clear on the fact that this helper He spoke about is to be comparable in other words equal to the man and is provided to support in accomplishing a task.

Have you ever tried to clean the house without any cleaning supplies? It is impossible. This is what God is saying about the value of women. They are a very critical piece to the task men were assigned. That is why God further tells us in the book of Genesis that He could not find a suitable mate for man, and after the creation of woman; God rested. His work was complete. What I find interesting when studying this particular scripture is that the opposite of support is hindrance. This is intriguing because in some ways it feels that the word support has been negated from the role of women and replaced with its antonym of hindrance.

Reading further into Genesis; God clearly continues explaining how valuable the creation of woman is. *And the Lord God caused a deep sleep to fall on Adam, and he slept; and he took one of his ribs, and closed up the flesh in its place. (22) Then the rib which the Lord God had taken from the man He made into woman, and He brought her to the man. (Genesis 2:21-22 NKJV)* This passage outlines a series of events, from where woman came from to how woman was presented to man.

God took a rib from man, went away, hand crafted woman and brought her to the man. Normally, when you are bringing something to someone else that they did not already have possession of and doesn't require payment for, it is considered a gift. It would be safe to say that woman was created as a gift to man. That is a bold statement. While I was facilitating a Bible study which consisted of teenage girls, one of the girls said, in a cynical and prideful way, "I am a gift." Quickly, I found myself addressing her statement. As I explained to her I will say the same here, it is okay to believe you are a gift to man, however that is a strong title to hold too. This means as a woman we have to walk in that gifted-ness. When someone is given a gift, a majority of the time it is something that is intended to bring them joy and a smile to their face. Nonetheless, there are times we receive gifts that we truly wish we could return; however most gifts have the intention to bring the receiver a sense of happiness.

Being a gift requires a gift mentality. We see a great example of what it means to be a gift in Proverbs 31. The Proverbs 31 woman, found in the Holy Bible, is the most common biblical passage that is utilized in defining the role of women. This passage, from the surface, describes how to be a mother, housekeeper, and a wife. However, when reading deeper into this passage it uncovers much more than the obvious. The woman described in this passage is well-rounded; educated, smart, prosperous, enthusiastic, hardworking, selfless, a problem solver, a critical thinker, she is respected, goal minded, and creative. Those are some pretty big shoes to fill. The last verse of Proverbs 31 concludes by describing her as being honored and praised for her work. Now that is what God created when He created this remarkable creation called "woman." "Who can find a virtuous and capable wife? She is more precious than rubies. Her husband can trust her, and she will greatly enrich his life. She brings him good, and not harm, all days of her life. She finds wool and flax and busily spins it. She is like a merchant's ship, bringing her food from afar. She gets up before dawn to prepare breakfast for her household and plan the day's work for her servant girls. She goes to inspect a field and buys it; with her earnings she plants a vineyard. She is energetic and strong, a hard worker. She makes sure her dealings are profitable; her lamp burns late into the night. Her hands are busy spinning thread, her fingers twisting fiber. She extends a helping hand to the poor and opens her arms to the needy. She has no fear of winter for her household, for everyone has warm clothes. She makes her own bedspreads. She dresses in fine linen and purple gowns. Her husband is well known at the city gates, where he sits with the other civic leaders. She makes belted linen garments and sashes to sell to the merchants. She is clothed with strength and dignity, and she laughs without fear of the future. When she speaks, her words are wise, and she gives instructions with kindness. She carefully watched everything in her household and suffers nothing from laziness. Her children stand and bless her." (Proverbs 31:10-31 NKJV)

Recently, I had the opportunity to pick out a gift for a friend. I found myself excited and anxious at the same time. Initially, I wasn't sure what I was going to buy, however for some reason I ended up in front of the watch counter. I began to think about the watch I had noticed my friend wearing previously and remembered that it was a pretty nice watch. I began to think that it would be a great idea if I bought a casual watch as a gift. The lady at the counter was very helpful as we stood there looking at watch after watch. I made sure there wasn't a flaw or even a finger print on the one I picked. At one point I even placed a watch on my wrist to determine if it would look too feminine. Nonetheless, after about the 12th watch, I found it; the perfect one. I hurried up and purchased it as if someone were going to attack me and take it. Ultimately I was extremely happy to have found the perfect gift.

This is an example of how critical picking out a gift can be and is used as an example of how significant and precious the creation of woman is. God went away in the Garden of Eden, created and hand crafted her, then He brought the woman to the man. The amount of care and diligence I put into picking out the perfect gift for a friend could not ever compare to the time, effort, and love that God put into creating His precious daughter. She was hand created, like a potter at a potter's wheel who strategically shaped and created the perfect pottery. She was made perfect. God did not make a mistake when He created her. He knew what he was doing and why. He even knew how valuable she would be in the present and future of mankind.

CHAPTER 3

MARTHA, MARTHA DO YOU HEAR ME?

*I*n the book of Luke 10:38-42; a woman named Martha is depicted as expressing her frustration with her sister Mary, regarding Jesus. Mary had refused to participate in domestic service which frustrated Martha. This resulted in Jesus responding to Martha in a way that was unexpected, and somehow condoned Mary's behavior to reject domestic service. Jesus was condoning Mary's behavior because she took the time to spend with Him and to hear what He was teaching her whereas Martha was distracted with the cares of the world. In no way is Jesus saying to us that we should neglect our responsibilities. He is telling us that there is a time for everything and spending time with Him is critical and should be a priority. Jesus even said to Martha; *Martha, Martha, you are worried and troubled about many things. But one thing is needed, and Mary has chosen that good*

part, which will not be taken away from her (Luke 10:41-42 NKJV)

Over the years, I have noticed through my own experiences and watching my women friends and acquaintances, is that we get absorbed in taking care of our homes; our children and our spouse's needs, and being a good employee and friend. We become so busy with life that we forget the most critical part to it, Jesus. I'm not saying that we negate who He is, what I am saying is that we get busy with life that we don't make Him the priority. Somehow we feel that because we are engulfed in serving that it becomes the priority and we feel that this service is what our Heavenly Father expects and wants from us. His expectation from us is that we put Him first. He wants us to get to know Him. All the other things in life are to follow after we take the time to build a relationship with Him.

Jesus said in the passage to Martha that *Mary has chosen that good part, which will not be taken away from her. (Luke 10:42 NKJV)* Jesus was telling Martha that the material things in this world can be taken away, yet Jesus is the good part of her life and He will never be taken away from her. If we looked at our relationship with Him from this perspective, would we value it a little more? Would we spend more time with Him? I am guilty of neglecting my relationship with Him therefore I understand the determination and mindfulness it takes to build and continue to have a relationship with Him.

One way I have found that has helped to make my relationship with Christ a priority is how I interpret my relationship with Him. He is my Lord and Heavenly Father and I had to think of Him also as my best friend. I had to change the way I was trained to think of Him. God has always been portrayed as this BIG, mean man who would send me to Hell in an instant and whom I should fear. Somehow that fear deterred my relationship with God and encouraged my continued disobedience.

Through this journey, God has revealed to me that He is not the "boogey man" many have portrayed Him to be. He, in fact, is the BEST example of a father, husband and friend anyone could ever have. He cares about His children and truly wants the BEST for them even in the midst of their own decisions. He protects us and hears our cries and our prayers and wants to take our cares, worry, and fears away from us. When I began to see God for who He is; I began to communicate with Him as a child to her father, a wife to her husband, and a friend to a friend.

One day I had received some good news and was so excited, I did what most people do, I picked up the phone to call a friend. Unfortunately my friend did not answer, so I called another friend, who did not answer either. As I hung up the phone I began to feel the excitement slipping away. At that moment I heard a gentle voice say; "You can share it with me," I began to smile and just began sharing the good news I had received, with the Heavenly Father. Can you imagine seeing someone driving down the street having a full conversation with hand gestures included? Well that was me. For those few minutes I was submerged in a conversation with my Heavenly Father. At that moment, I was comforted and reminded that He was the source of the joyful moment and what better way to show gratitude and gratefulness, than to share it with the one who made it all possible, God?

Chapter 4

MIND OVER MATTER

Another intriguing encounter between Jesus and a woman is the Samaritan woman at the well in John 4, NKJV.

"Therefore, when the Lord knew that the Pharisees had heard that Jesus made and baptized more disciples than John [2] (though Jesus Himself did not baptize, but His disciples), [3] He left Judea and departed again to Galilee. [4] But He needed to go through Samaria. [5] So He came to a city of Samaria which is called Sychar, near the plot of ground that Jacob gave to his son Joseph. [6] Now Jacob's well was there. Jesus therefore, being wearied from *His* journey, sat thus by the well. It was about the sixth hour. [7] A woman of Samaria came to draw water. Jesus said to her, 'Give Me a drink.' [8] For His disciples had gone away into the city to buy food. [9] Then the woman of Samaria said to Him, 'How is it that You, being a Jew, ask a drink from me, a Samaritan woman?' For Jews have no dealings with Samaritans. [10] Jesus answered and said to her, 'If you knew the gift of God, and who it is who says to you, 'Give Me a drink,' you would have asked Him, and He would have given you living water.' [11] The woman said to Him, 'Sir, You have nothing to draw with, and the well is deep. Where then do You get that living water? [12] Are You greater than our father Jacob, who gave us the well, and drank from it himself, as well as his sons and his livestock?' [13] Jesus answered and said to her, 'Whoever drinks of this water will thirst again, [14] but whoever drinks of the water that I shall give him will never thirst. But the water that I shall give him will become in him a fountain of water springing up into everlasting life.' [15] The woman said to Him, 'Sir, give me this water, that I may not thirst, nor come here to draw.' [16] Jesus said to her, 'Go, call your husband, and come here.' [17] The woman answered and said, 'I have no husband.' Jesus said to her, 'You have well said, 'I have no husband,' [18] for you have had five husbands, and the one whom you now have is not your husband; in that you spoke truly.' [19] The woman said to Him, 'Sir, I perceive that You are a prophet. [20] Our fathers worshiped on this mountain, and you *Jews* say that in Jerusalem is the place where one ought to worship.' [21] Jesus said to her, 'Woman, believe Me, the hour is coming when you will neither on this mountain, nor in Jerusalem, worship the Father. [22] You worship what you do not know; we know what we worship, for salvation is of the Jews. [23] But the hour is coming, and now is, when the true worshipers will worship the Father in spirit and truth; for the Father is seeking such to worship Him. [24] God *is* Spirit, and those who worship Him must worship in spirit and truth.'[25] The woman said to Him, 'I know that Messiah is coming (who is called Christ). When He comes, He will tell us all things.'[26] Jesus said to her, 'I who speak to you am *He*.'[27] And at this *point* His disciples came, and they marveled that He talked with a woman; yet no one said, 'What do You seek?' or, 'Why are You talking with her?'[28] The woman then left her waterpot, went her way into the city, and said to the men, [29] 'Come, see a Man who told me all things that I ever did. Could this be the Christ?'[30] Then they went out of the city and came to Him."

I wonder what could have been going on in the Samaritan woman's mind. Initially, she had no idea that she was having a conversation with Jesus; therefore she probably did not think much about it. In this story, we read that Jesus sat at the well and the woman approached to draw water. Jesus asked the woman for a drink. She immediately reminded Jesus that she was a Samaritan woman and He was a Jew. Intriguingly, during this era, Samaritans and Jews despised one another even though these two tribes came from the same father, Joseph. Now Jesus did not tell her who He was; however He did say to her in a loving way that if she knew who He was she would have asked Him for a drink and without hesitation He would have given her living water. She was so blinded by the world in which she lived in and the rituals of the time that she did not understand what Jesus was offering. Jesus kindly informed her that the water from the well that she drinks from (the world) would leave her thirsty, but with the water from the well of Jesus she would never thirst again and she would have everlasting life.

When she heard this she yearned for what Jesus was offering and asked Him for it. At this moment Jesus asked her to get her husband. This is interesting because He is Jesus and He knew her situation. He knew it so well that He told her how many husbands she did have right after she acknowledged she had no current husband, AND the man she was currently with was not her husband. Her skeletons were out of the closet and yet she thought Jesus was merely a prophet. At the end of her encounter with Jesus; He identified to her who He was, at which time she was left to tell others about her experience and in turn stirred up a yearning inside of those she told.

This story intrigues me so much that I have even found myself wondering what I would feel, think, or say if I were the Samaritan woman. She found herself in a debate with Jesus and still did not know who she encountered until Jesus told her. He found it critical for the people (unworthy people according to society, like the Samaritans) to know who He was and not for His benefit yet for theirs. After the Samaritan woman's encounter with Jesus she went to the rest of the people in Samaria and shared what she had experienced. Through her sharing of her testimony to others, they became eager to hear and see Jesus and ultimately, many were saved.

The most profound understanding to take away from the Samaritan Woman's story is that the Lord offers salvation to everyone, even those with unfavorable past, whom society deems insufficient or unworthy and that our testimony can help positively impact the lives of others. During the time of this encounter, Samaritans were those individuals seen as unworthy, yet the Savior was willing to save them and give them eternal life despite who they were. He did not see the Samaritan woman the same way others in society saw her. He wanted a relationship with her and even went as far as to tell her who He was because He saw her worthy to save.

One thing to remember is that in moments of doubt; God created us uniquely special and it is Satan's plan to keep us in bondage over our past sins. That is not what God has said in His word, in fact He makes it clear that when we accept Him as our Savior and ask for forgiveness we are made new; *Therefore, if anyone is in Christ, he is a new creation; old things have passed away; behold, all things have become new. (2 Corinthians 5:17 NKJV)* In this scripture, God did not say that only some things are made new; He said ALL things. When we seek forgiveness from Him, He forgives us and He no longer sees our sins. Therefore, the sins of our past that are on replay in our minds are from none other than Satan, whose plan and desire is for us to be in a place that prevents us from moving forward. These negative thoughts leave us feeling like we are in quicksand and no one is there to help us get out of it. We then begin to feel so weak that we develop a feeling of unworthiness that eliminates our desire to be what God has planned for us to be.

From the beginning of our creation; Satan has used our minds as his primary way of attacking us, causing confusion and ultimately hindering our ability to pursue God's purpose for our lives. When we are able to identify where the attack is coming from, then we will be able to utilize the right armor when preparing for the battle. Let's look back at the events that transpired in the Garden of Eden. *Now the Serpent was more cunning than any beast of the field which the Lord God had made. And he said to the woman, "Has God indeed said 'You shall not eat of every tree of the Garden?" (Genesis 3:1 NKJV)* This is interesting because Satan had to ask Eve what God had instructed of her, yet he knew what God had instructed them to not eat, as we see through his question. *And the woman said to the serpent, "We may eat the fruit of the trees of the garden; but of the fruit of the tree which is in the midst of the garden, God has said, "You shall not eat it, nor shall you touch it, lest you die."' Then the serpent said to the woman, "You will not surely die. For God knows that in the day you eat of it your eyes will be opened, and you will be like God, knowing good and evil." So when the woman saw that the tree was good for food, that it was pleasant to the eyes, and a tree desirable to make one wise, she took of its fruit and ate. She also gave to her husband with her, and he ate. Then the eyes of both of them were opened, and they knew that they were naked; and they sewed fig leaves together and made themselves coverings. (Genesis 3:2-7 NKJV)*

Satan went straight to Eve, not Adam, to get her to betray the instructions God had given. He had a plan to confuse Eve. He was cunning. He knew exactly the right words to say to Eve to get her to be disobedient to God and immediately after Adam had eaten the fruit, their eyes were opened. Anxiety and fear began to overwhelm them and they began to worry. They frantically scurried to put clothes on as they acknowledged their nakedness. They even hid as God approached. When I read about their reaction, it was a serious reaction yet I can't help but laugh because this reaction would be similar to a newborn baby hiding from his or her parent. I think God is fully aware of what He created and what we look like in our nakedness.

As God asked what happened (He already knew, He wanted them to tell Him), Adam began by blaming Eve. This was the beginning of a communication breakdown between God and man and between man and woman. God was not keeping them away from this specific area of the garden for His best interest, but for theirs. He was trying to protect them from sin and disobedience which leads to spiritual death. He was trying to keep them safe while Satan was waiting to find the perfect moment to destroy their relationship and the relationship between them and God.

Another valid point to make regarding the Garden of Eden is the critical and incapacitating effect that anxiety, fear, doubt, and worry can play in our lives. In my professional life, I have had the pleasure of meeting and speaking to many women who have discussed with me their struggles with these particular feelings. This leads me to believe that Satan has not changed his tactics and we must remember that anxiety and fear are not from God. In fact, anxiety, fear, doubt, and worry are unhealthy for us. These characteristics can also weaken our immune systems by the very things they produce like the lack of sleep, and unhealthy and unproductive habits that develop.

Anxiety and fear lead us to focus on ourselves and our problems. We then tend to negate other responsibilities in our lives and forget that the Heavenly Father instructed us to love others. When we begin feeling anxiety, doubt, worry, and fear; if we would redirect those feelings into a more constructive and positive feeling like love, we could see those characteristics for what they really are. For example: calling a friend – not for advice, but to see if they need help with something, or maybe getting involved in the community and volunteering, or by merely giving our time to something other than the negative thought (read the Bible). As a result, of taking the energy to focus on others and not ourselves, we would see that the anxiety, fear, doubt or worry are not there to help us but to incapacitate us from the joy and peace God has for us.

Have you ever done something for someone else and experienced the feelings of selflessness and love and as a result you forgot all about your own difficulties or struggles? God wants us to experience His peace, joy, and love by doing the opposite of what anxiety, doubt, worry, and fear would have us do. The word of God tells us; *Be anxious for nothing, but in everything by prayer and supplication, with thanksgiving, let your request be made known to God. (Philippians 4:6 NKJV)* And; *Therefore do not worry about tomorrow, for tomorrow will worry about its own things. Sufficient for the day is its own trouble. (Matthew 6:34 NKJV)*

Fear, doubt, anxiety, and worry are feelings that can critically incapacitate our minds and develop based on "a thought" that enters our mind. Therefore, if Satan can implant these negative thoughts into our minds; we will begin to feel unworthy and devalued and settle for mediocrity. This means that we do not feel motivated or determined to strive for who God says we are or the authority that God says we walk in. Nor do we align our lives with His plans for our lives; we settle for the riches we can acquire on our own and never really reach our God given potential for fear of stepping out of our comfort zone. This comfort zone we developed in the process of feeling not worthy enough or uncertain of God's plan for us, or we never really understood who God is and what He says about us.

For I know the plans I have for you," says the Lord. "They are plans for good and not for disaster, to give you a future and a hope. In those days when you pray, I will listen. If you look for me wholeheartedly, you will find me. (Jeremiah 29:11-13 NLT)

CHAPTER 5

THE POWER IN THE WOMB

Then the angel said to her, "Do not be afraid, Mary, for you have found favor with God. And behold, you will conceive in your womb and bring forth a Son, and shall call His name JESUS. He will be great, and will be called the Son of the Highest; and the Lord God will give Him the throne of His father David." (Luke 1:30-32 NKJV)

Often times when the story of Mary is told, Mary's critical role in being a key component in our salvation is somehow overlooked or quickly brushed over. Mary was a teenage virgin who the Lord found favor in. He did not just place Jesus, our Lord and Savior of the World, into her. He actually sent the angel Gabriel to her and asked her if she would be willing to accept Jesus into her womb. At sixteen years old what could she have known about raising a child? However she, at sixteen, had enough faith to listen to the angel about the child she would carry. In spite of any backlash and hatred remarks she would receive from society about her being a pregnant teenage girl and being unmarried; she took a step of faith and agreed to walk in her purpose.

This must have been a frightful time for her initially. Nonetheless, Mary was comforted by the angel Gabriel and ultimately gave birth to the Savior. The SAVIOR! That is huge. God picked a woman, a teenage girl, to bring the Savior into the world. He picked a woman to contribute to His mission and save ALL. Looking at the mere fact that a teenage girl that had no significance, according to the society at the time; she brought Jesus into the world. Understanding the life of Mary and her obedience is critical when understanding the value and worth of women, according to God. He gave her the opportunity to decide if she would trust Him and step out in faith in spite of any obstacles. She had to believe that God was going to take care of her throughout her pregnancy and her life.

Now indeed, Elizabeth your relative has also conceived a son in her old age; and this is now the sixth month for her who was called barren. (Luke 1:36 NKJV)

Prior to Mary conceiving Jesus, one of her relatives became pregnant. This woman was named Elizabeth. She was an older woman who had previously been told she could not have children. Despite her age and her inability to bear children, the angel Gabriel visited Elizabeth's husband, Zacharias, who was well aged too. The Angel of the Lord told Elizabeth's husband that she was going to conceive a child and name him John. This child later did great things for the Kingdom of God, in fact he lead the way for the introduction of Jesus, The Savior. Again, we see that God shows us the importance of the role of women and their significant purposes to the Kingdom of God through the life of Elizabeth.

It was not until Elizabeth was in her sixth month of pregnancy that Jesus was placed in Mary's womb. When it came time for Elizabeth to give birth, she did, and all her neighbors and family rejoiced with her. Elizabeth became a pillar of hope. Her circumstances said she was not able to bear children and yet she had given birth to a baby by the grace of God. Can you imagine what people must have thought as this older woman was giving birth despite the fact that she was called barren? When she delivered her baby, I can imagine the reactions of the other women in the community.

On the eighth day after Elizabeth gave birth, her neighbors and family suggested that the child be named after his father. Elizabeth earnestly disagreed. Her neighbors and friends then suggested the father provide his opinion to what the child's name should be. This is an interesting insert in the scripture because in the beginning of Elizabeth's pregnancy, the angel Gabriel was instructed by the Holy Spirit, to shut Zacharias mouth. Therefore, Zacharias could not talk to his pregnant wife or to anyone else. However, when he was asked about the name of his child, he actually spoke and said John, the same name Elizabeth said. They were obedient to God's instructions.

The people had to be in a state of shock for two reasons; one reason had to be that Elizabeth did not give the child her husband's name and the other is that Zacharias picked the same name as her, after months of muteness. Normally, during the process of preparing for a baby there is usually some kind of discussion about the name of the child. In this instance, we see Elizabeth's and Zacharias's obedience in naming their child. Her family and friends began to talk, saying they wondered what will come of a boy with this type of name. I wonder as time progressed, what was going through their minds as John grew and became a powerful man of God?

Mary and Elizabeth carried some of the most inspirational and fundamental servant leaders. Elizabeth's womb carried a man by the name of John the Baptist and the child conceived in Mary's womb was a man named Jesus. Two instrumental men, within the Bible, came from two women that the world would have seen as insufficient; one that was a barren woman and one that was a teenage unwed virgin girl.

While Jesus was living in the Galilean hills, John, called "the Baptizer," was preaching in the desert country of Judea. His message was simple and austere, like his desert surroundings: "Change your life. God's kingdom is here." John and his message were authorized by Isaiah's prophecy: "Thunder in the desert! Prepare for God's arrival! Make the road smooth and straight!" John dressed in a camel-hair habit tied at the waist by a leather strap. He lived on a diet of locusts and wild field honey. People poured out of Jerusalem, Judea, and the Jordanian countryside to hear and see him in action. There at the Jordan River those who came to confess their sins were baptized into a changed life. When John realized that a lot of Pharisees and Sadducees were showing up for a baptismal experience because it was becoming the popular thing to do, he exploded: "Brood of snakes! What do you think you're doing slithering down here to the river? Do you think a little water on your snakeskins is going to make any difference? It's your life that must change, not your skin! And don't think you can pull rank by claiming Abraham as father. Being a descendant of Abraham is neither here nor there. Descendants of Abraham are a dime a dozen. What counts is your life. Is it green and blossoming? Because if it's deadwood, it goes on the fire. I'm baptizing you here in the river, turning your old life in for a kingdom life. The real action comes next: The main character in this drama—compared to him I'm a mere stagehand—will ignite the kingdom life within you, a fire within you, the Holy Spirit within you, changing you from the inside out. He's going to clean house—make a clean sweep of your lives. He'll place everything true in its proper place before God; everything false he'll put out with the trash to be burned." Jesus then appeared, arriving at the Jordan River from Galilee. He wanted John to baptize him. John objected, "I'm the one who needs to be baptized, not you!" But Jesus insisted. "Do it. God's work, putting things right all these centuries, is coming together right now in this baptism." So John did it. The moment Jesus came up out of the baptismal waters, the skies opened up and he saw God's Spirit—it looked like a dove—descending and landing on him. And along with the Spirit, a voice: "This is my Son, chosen and marked by my love, delight of my life." (Matthew 3:1-17 MSG)

CHAPTER 6

WHO AM I

So we are Christ's ambassadors; God is making his appeal through us. We speak for Christ when we plead, "Come back to God!" (2 Corinthians 5:20 NLT)

Let me start by saying that writing this book is written out of obedience and sharing this story is to encourage others. At the age of five, most children are enjoying playing with their siblings and beginning to broaden their understanding of the world by developing relationships/friendships with others. Unfortunately, at five I reflect on painful memories of living in a van, washing up in a pan, and watching my mother plead for her life while being beaten by my father. By the age of seventeen, I had scarcely survived the world of childhood homelessness, domestic violence, human trafficking, rape, anorexia, and alcoholism. By the time I had become an adult, I had become a product of my past and a victim of domestic violence.

After leaving an eleven year abusive relationship, I felt worthless, contemplated returning to the very man, for about the sixth time, who abused me. At one point I even thought about taking my own life. I felt hopeless and helpless and during this time I cried out to my Lord and Heavenly Father and asked Him; "Why am I here? Why do I even exist? Who am I?" My entire life had been worth nothing and those individuals who were closest to me had either abandoned me or told me I would never be anything. After asking the Heavenly Father those three fundamental questions; He answered and His answer would take me on a four year journey of restoration, healing, and being made new.

Over the course of those four years, God poured life back into me. He helped to restore my soul and to overcome the mental damage I had endured for thirty-three years. During this journey, I have come to realize that with a surrendered life; God can and will take the most unworthy, in society's eyes, and make them worthy. I was one of those that was deemed and classified as unworthy, by others and by my own standards. For many years, I was told I was nothing and I thought that my role as a woman was defined by what others thought and said about me and what my childhood had taught me about being a woman.

Now I believe God uses those who have been restored from; hurt, alcoholism, homelessness, prostitution, deceivers, doubters, adulterers, and even drug addicts, to share His grace and mercy with others. Before now, I thought these types of people, like me, were damned to Hell and could never be forgiven or at least never looked at as if we were like those who claim to not be sinners. I do not believe that the negative situations we find ourselves in are ever God's plan and purpose for our lives and many of these situations are a result of our actions or they stem from the actions of others. Nonetheless these acts are a result of our free will and God cannot and will not take our free will away however our free will choices can change when we are walking in a relationship with him. In no way am I blaming others, so please do not mistake what I am saying.

I have found that when we blame others for our problems, we end up in a mindset of being a victim and we have a harder time moving forward in life into a mindset of being a survivor. God has better plans for us and they are not to live in bondage, nor are they to live and be what society or anyone else have said about us. God created us to be masterpieces of Him. However, due to life circumstances and unfavorable paths we decided to take, our lives have not reflected our full potential in God's eyes. Nonetheless, God can and will restore us back to what His original plan was for us in the beginning of our creation.

CHAPTER 7

NOTHING CLOSE TO NORMAL

But Jesus refused to permit him, but said to him, "Go home to your own [family and relatives and friends] and bring back word to them of how much the Lord has done for you and [how He has] had sympathy for you and mercy on you."(Mark 5:19 AMP)

Childhood for me was far from normal. Some parts I remember clearly, as if they happened yesterday and some are just vague and cloudy. I was born on July 3, 1977, as my mother would put it–the year Elvis died. My mother is Caucasian and my father was African American. Growing up, when people asked me; "what are you?", as if I were other than human; I would respond "half black and half white." The older I became, the more I was able to truly identify my racial background, but as a child I thought my race was merely the color of my parent's skin.

Until the age of three, we lived in Fort Wayne, Indiana, where majority of my mom's side of the family still live today. I don't remember much about the first three years of my life or what it was like living in Indiana, however, my father shared stories with me about how prejudiced the people were and my mother told us the story about how her mother didn't accept that she had married a black man and had "nigger" babies. That may be why I never had the opportunity to meet my grandmother before she passed away.

My father was a truck driver for North American Van Lines. I'm not quite sure what my mother did for a living when she met my father. She is a pretty private person, as I have learned throughout the years. Shortly after meeting my father, my mother would give birth to my sister and then a few years later, she had me and three years later we moved to California.

As I stated previously, my memories of my early childhood are vivid, however I do remember at the age of four we lived in an apartment in Imperial Beach, California. The memories I have of living there were of one of my father's ways of making money. I would sometimes watch him weigh sandwich bags of marijuana and then we would drive around the beach area as scraggly individuals would walk up to the car and exchange money for little baggies of what looked like green weeds, later I learned that this was marijuana. I vaguely remember strange looking people discussing with my father what the smell of the marijuana meant.

Before my sixth birthday, our family moved from the apartment and began living in our van that consisted of only the front two seats. In the back of the van, we would lay blankets down at night to try to provide some cushion to make the metal floor not so uncomfortable to sleep on. If we had to use the restroom we had a stainless steel bowl that we would use and then empty it into the flower bed in the grocery store parking lot. We religiously parked in the same parking lot where we slept and woke up in, nearly every morning. We had a small television that plugged into the cigarette lighter and had an antenna on top. We did not get very many channels but Saturday mornings were always a treat because Saturday morning cartoons we always eagerly awaited for. I can recall Thunder Cats, He-Man and She-Ra being my favorite cartoons.

Around the age of six, I remember breaking the antenna on the television and my father being so angry at me. That day he stood in front of me with a belt in his hand, but not just any belt; this was the belt that slaves would get hit with (as he told me). I don't know where he got it from but I remember it was extremely thick. He told me to take off all my clothes and he put me face down on the floor. He then sat on my back so I wouldn't run away and he began hitting me on my bottom with that belt. Somehow, I managed to wiggle free and got out of the van and ran down the street. I'm not quite sure what happened after that because the memory seems to fade but overtime not much had changed.

The spankings became normal. If we did anything wrong in my father's eyes, we got hit with anything my father could get his hands on. I can remember being hit with an extension cord, the cord from the iron, belts, tree branches and even the whip that horses are hit with. I can recall going to school daily with welt marks on my legs, back, and bottom; that it just became normal. I would still wear dresses despite the marks showing. I'm not sure if any of my teachers ever noticed but they never asked and at the time I did not think it was unusual. I thought all kids got spankings; they just never talked about it.

My life outside of school consisted of playing with Cabbage Patch Kids and Barbie dolls. As I reflect back, I believe mentally I escaped reality, through playing with these dolls, and somehow went into another world; the world of my Barbie dolls and Cabbage Patch Kids. This imaginary world contributed to my lack of completing my homework and schoolwork and while I was in the third grade, my assignments and homework began to stack up on my desk. The stack had to be about a foot tall and sat on the corner of my desk. My teacher's solution to this was to keep me in from recess and separating me from my classmates, so I could focus on my assignments. This didn't matter much to me because I didn't have many friends. While at school, most of the time, I played by myself or with the one friend I had. I remember her because she was kind.

When I was able to play outside, I recall playing in the sandbox alone or that one friend would find me and we would play together. Approximately Half way through the school year, I finished the assignment in that stack on my desk. I wasn't too excited about it because I had to face the one boy on the playground who I had a crush on. He made fun of me, teasing me and saying my butt was on my back, as all the other kids would laugh at me. Unfortunately, the same boy stayed at the same school throughout elementary, middle school, and the beginning of my high school years. His teasing never really changed, he just added to it as I went up in grades to beginning to tease me for being "flat chested." His teasing continued up to high school. The crush I had on him shortly changed more to hate by about the fourth grade. I could not stand being around him and I found myself trying to stay away from him and his friends on a daily basis. This wasn't easy because it seemed that the more he made fun of me, the more friends he developed. All I could do was cry but not around him or any of his fan club. I did not want him to see that he was hurting me for fear he would use that to tease me with later.

Despite not having a place to call home I do remember my father driving us to the Los Angeles garment district where we would each get close to $200. This was the money to buy our school clothes for the year. I recall always picking out dresses and at least one pair of dress shoes. I wanted to feel and look like a pretty little "normal" girl. There were times I wanted to tell someone that my family lived in our car. But I never did because I didn't want to feel the humiliation that I was different. I at least knew that living in a van was not normal. Our van was the place we called home until I believe I was in the 6th grade. By that time, my mother and father became self-employed and we sold miscellaneous used items at the swap meet.

Eventually, we went from selling used items to selling new items. The stuff we first sold at the swap meet came from the blue goodwill boxes that random people would put their donated items into. I remember my mother crawling into the blue bin and sorting through it to find items that we could sell and items that we could use. One day, I remember we came across 10-12 boxes of meals ready to eat (MRE's) that someone had left next to the Goodwill box. This was a blessing for us because these would be the meals that my parents gave us for a few weeks. Normally, our meals consisted of my father giving us a dollar, maybe every other day, which we had two options, jack-in-the box tacos or a piece of bread from the bakery. The deli always seemed too expensive yet I remember walking in there and just sitting for a few minutes. At one point my older sister and I decided to put our dollars together and we shared what we ordered. It made the portions somehow seem bigger.

My parent's self-employment became our main source of income for about two years. I do not ever recall my father digging in those blue bins, maybe because it was something that he felt was belittling for him, but not too belittling for my mother to do. After a couple of years, my father met a man who gave him the idea to sell pillows at the swap meet. So he did. I remember our family driving to Los Angeles three to four times a week so my father could pick up pillows from a factory to resell. These trips were always fun because there were other children that we could play with and we occasionally stopped at our cousins house, ate, and played. My father at some point bought a second van so we could store the pillows we were selling and the first van was still used for us to live in. Now there were two vans parked in the grocery store parking lot and no one ever asked us to move or if we needed help.

My family living in our car, and us being beaten wasn't the only secrets we were keeping; our father was beating our mom regularly. I can remember lying on the floor of the van pretending I was sleep and hearing my mother cry and beg for my father to stop hitting her. There were several times I could recall when my mother would drive us somewhere and an argument would begin. My father would punch my mother at which time she would become unconscious and my father would somehow pull her out of the driver's seat and manage to take over driving. My older sister and I would cry because we never knew if our mother was alive until she regained consciousness. I think this became a game for my father because it occurred more and more frequently as time progressed. For a majority of my childhood our van was where we called home but one day the owner of the swap meet was kind enough to buy a trailer in a trailer park and let my parents rent it from him. After moving into the trailer, I thought we would somehow become that "normal" family. I believed we would be like all the families I watched on television like, The Cosby's and The Cleaver's, but what did I know?

Chapter 8

TILL DEATH DO US PART

*M*oving into the trailer park provided us with a physical home to call our own; however, things never really changed much. In fact, they seemed to get worse. As I reflect back; I remember never being able to play outside with other children. I can recall sitting on the porch playing with my Barbie's and watching the other children run around chasing one another. One day, I decided to invite one of the little girls in the neighborhood to come over and play with me and she did. I remember my father calling me back into the house and spanking me because I had her come over to play with me. His spankings were so hard and terrifying they made me wish I wasn't alive. His punishment was not a friendly time-out or a smack on the bottom with a hand. His punishment made you never want to get into trouble but it never seemed to fail; I was destined to receive a spanking. I wonder if he ever felt guilty for being so harsh to us or if he even realized how cruel he was.

My father never talked much about his childhood and the little he did share was about segregation and the price of tangible material items when he was younger. It wasn't until my mid 30's that I found out my father's family dynamics. My mother told me that my father was taken away from his mother shortly after birth by his father, who took him to his grandmother to be raised. I vaguely remember my great grandmother when I was a toddler. The memory I have of her is of her peeing on the kitchen floor and my mother cleaning it up. It wasn't until later that my mother shared with me that my great grandmother disliked her because she was a white woman and she was married to my father.

Living in the trailer was a new place to call home and seemed far better than the van. The beatings and the violence in our household never stopped however at least we had an actual roof over our heads. Tragically, shortly after we began living there, my father began sexually abusing me. When my mother was informed it did not appear as though she believed me. I don't know what my mother did with the information, however; about a month later, I was sitting on the couch watching television and I heard a knock at the door. I got up and answered it. There was a man standing there and he asked me if my parents were home. I called for my dad and he came to the door, at which time the man asked my dad to step outside. As I continued to watch, I noticed there were police officers standing on the porch, placing my dad in handcuffs and directing him down the stairs. As my dad was escorted down the stairs the man began talking to my mom. The more I watched; the more nervous and scared I became. I began to cry.

My father was put into the back of the police car. My siblings and I were placed into another car and driven to a center where we slept on cots with a blanket. I remember being cold, scared, and crying most of the night. We had been removed from our parents' custody and placed into foster care. I was devastated. It felt like we were torn away from our parents without explanation and no one asked us what was going on in our home that I can recall.

My three siblings and I were placed in a foster home with an older African American woman and her husband. Our foster parents had adult children of their own that did not live with them. We slept on bunk beds with two of us in each room. Our routine over the first thirty days with this couple consisted of watching airplanes land and take off at the airport, daily, as we waited for our foster-father to get off from work. We had meals daily, a nice roof over our head, and I was with my siblings. Sometime over the course of the 30 days we lived with them, my younger two siblings were separated from my sister and I and went to live with our foster parent's daughter. This stay was very brief for my younger siblings due to my brother sustaining a burn while their new foster parent was cooking. This triggered my older sister and I to be removed from our foster parents care and placed in another foster home. I am uncertain where my younger two siblings were moved to after this home; however I do know they were moved.

For roughly another month or two, our new foster parent was a single woman who was a light skin African American woman with adult children. She worked a full-time job and when she went to work she took us to the local Boys and Girls Club. Living with her was one of the best experiences I can recall in my childhood. I was able to be a part of social activities. I was able to play with other kids. I was able to be a part of something aside from chaos and pain. I was afforded the opportunity to build friendships. My sister and I tried out for the cheerleading and flag team and we made the teams. Having the opportunity to be around other kids our age gave me a sense of belonging and the ability to grow socially. I did not understand or have many relationships with peers up until this point in my life. I also believe that the color of her skin played a significant part in my feelings of completeness. We were raised by a black father and a white mother therefore our upbringing was not conclusive of that to an all black family or an all white family. Living with the first foster family I remember not feeling like I was a part of a family yet the second foster parent I did.

After these months in foster care my mother came and picked us up one day. We were told by her that we were going back to live with her. I remember being filled with so much happiness and joy. I think my smile could have lit up a dark street for miles. We were all back together again, except for my father. My mother explained to us that my father was not allowed to live with us any longer or to be around us. At the time, I didn't really understand why, however, as time passed; I began to understand that the way in which my father treated us was unhealthy, to say the least. This separation became a struggle for my father. I would see him periodically in the grocery store parking lot across the street from where we lived.

I rode my bike to the grocery store when my mom would need something and many times my dad would be in the parking lot and call me over to his van where he would hug me and tell me that he loved me. I remember going to the parking lot frequently just to see if my dad was there. Now I understand a little better why my father was in the grocery store parking lot. It appears that my father was stalking my mother. Why else would he frequently be nearby a home he could not reside in?

My mom began developing friends within the trailer park that we lived in and eventually started dating a man who was in the Navy. The more she got involved with him, the more I would see my father in the neighborhood. One day, my mother was at our neighbor's house with her friends, we (my siblings and I) were at home. All of the sudden, I saw my father climbing into the back bedroom window. As he entered he told me to go get my mom. I went to the neighbor's house and I told my mom that dad was in the house and wanted her. As she came out of the neighbor's house, my father began running down the street with my younger sister in his arms. My mom began chasing after my father, who at some point put my younger sister down in the middle of the street My mom called the police and they arrived shortly after that encounter, nonetheless, I did not know that this would be the last time I was going to see my father.

These events occurred during the summer and did not affect attendance in our schooling. When I returned to school, I was beginning middle school. Approximately three months into middle school I sprained my wrist and the nurse called my neighbor because she could not reach my mother. My neighbor came and picked me up from school. As we drove home, I asked her "where is my mom?" She replied, "Your mom had to go to Los Angeles and take care of something." As I looked over at her I asked, "What, did my dad die?" She replied "Yes." I was in shock and I have no idea why I said what I said. At that moment I can only recall opening the door as she came to a stop sign and I got out of the car and started walking. That was the last thing I wanted to happen to my dad, so why did I say it? At that moment, I had an array of thoughts that came rushing into my mind. I truly felt as if my life had ended and it wasn't fair. I became numb.

My father had four boys and one girl from two previous relationships that we did not know much about, growing up. By the time our father passed away, these five children were adults. So when he passed away, four of the five became involved and came to our house to divide my father's belongings and help with his funeral arrangements. My father's funeral was a somber experience. His casket was opened only for a short time and had to be closed, due to the smell. My father had been deceased for a week before he was found. After a week of his van sitting in a Church's Chicken parking lot, his van was towed and when the tow truck driver opened the van he found my father's body lying in the back. It is my understanding that my father had a heart attack. For years after my father had passed away, there have been speculations within my family, that his death was not the result of natural causes as reported.

CHAPTER 9

POWER AND CONTROL VS. LOVE

There is therefore now no condemnation to those who are in Christ Jesus, who do not walk according to the flesh, but according to the Spirit. For the law of the Spirit of life in Christ Jesus has made me free from the law of sin and death. (Romans 8:1-2 NKJV)

After the loss of my father and the devastation that shook my life shortly before his death; I believe the next series of events that occurred in my life are attributed to these past events. I felt lost and like nothing mattered. I felt invisible and could not wait to grow up. I found myself in bad relationship after bad relationship, giving my body away and trying to fill a void that never seemed to get filled; no matter how hard I tried. My mother and step-father tried their best to raise the four of us, however; I think the difficult part was that my step-father was ten years younger than my mom and did not have any idea of how to raise children. He had none of his own and my mother never had to really raise us because my father took that role from her.

My step-father was in the United States Navy and tried extremely hard to instill in us characteristics of integrity and determination. He tried to provide us with a nice home and structure which was difficult to understand because we weren't used to structure. We were used to being raised in a home of fear and control. However, at the time when we really needed our mother to guide us and love us, it seemed like he took her away from us. This caused a feeling of abandonment even though neither of them hadn't a clue that this feeling even existed and prompted my search for the love I desired.

At the age of fifteen years old, I ran away from home out of rebellion toward my step-father. I thought I could do everything on my own. I often found myself saying, "Who does he think he is? He isn't my father." One day after my step father said, "If you don't like my rules, then you can leave." I did just that, I left. I took most of my clothes and eventually moved into my best friend's house. I thought this was the best decision of my life. I was able to drink alcohol, go wherever I wanted to, and stay out as long as I wanted to. This was the life, so I thought. Within weeks I found myself in the arms of a man that made promises to me of an easy and wealthy lifestyle. In reality, it was an easy and rich lifestyle for him. However, it cost me dignity, humility, self-esteem and at times I felt like I had sold my soul to the devil himself. I desperately sought to be loved and would do anything and believed anything to have it. I had no idea that the love I was seeking actually would be the love that would cost me a lengthy life of emptiness.

I found myself on a roadway that led me to one unhealthy relationship after another. I was searching to be loved and to fill the emptiness and void that my father left when he passed away. I got into a relationship with a man who was ten years older than me. This relationship put me into a dark world of beatings, rape, alcoholism, anorexia, and human trafficking. To take the pain away and numb what was happening to me; I became an alcoholic and then developed anorexia as a way to control some aspect of my life. I sustained several beatings and at one point I was beaten so severely, that I was unrecognizable. I had been burned with an iron and raped twice; once at gun point and another time at knife point. I had been beaten with a shotgun and had a knife and a pencil forced into my chest.

During this specific beating, I thought I was going to die and had been instructed to lie down on a white sheet. I was told that I was going to be wrapped in the sheet and thrown out of the car, onto the freeway. At that moment, I prayed and asked God to let me die to end the pain. The knife and pencil never penetrated my skin during the first attempt to end my life. During the second attempt, involving the shotgun, a newscast came across the television about the murder of Nicole Brown – Simpson, which deterred my abusers from ending my life.

The odd thing is; during this time in my life, I found myself singing Amazing Grace at the strangest moments. This was odd to me because I was not raised in the Church nor did I truly have a complete or clear understanding of God. Growing up, my father would take us to a Catholic Church that we attended only on holidays like Easter and Christmas. I recall thinking, as a child, how silly it was that people would dip their fingers in this pan when entering Church and say a set of rehearsed prayers.

I had no real understanding of what the prayer meant. My connection with Church would end from the time I was eleven or twelve until roughly about the age of thirteen. At thirteen, my older sister introduced me to a Christian Church. I enjoyed attending as it made me feel like I was a part of something, however, I still did not understand what or who God was. One day while at Church, I do recall asking Jesus to come into my heart, however not much changed in my life and I don't recall ever really understanding what I had done. Therefore, when I was enduring such a destructive life I'm not quite sure where the desire to sing Amazing Grace even came from. Perhaps it was a hymn I had once sang in the Christian Church.

After six month of living in this dark world, I managed to escape after being held hostage in a hotel room for a week. Eventually, I ended up back home and within the first 24 hours my parents thought it would be in my best interest to go to a residential treatment center. While I was there, I was diagnosed with Battered Women's Syndrome, anorexia, and depression. Despite the psychologists desire to have me take an antidepressant medication; I refused. I made this decision because I did not feel as if I was depressed and more so that the situation I had just left was making me depressed.

I stayed in this treatment center for five months. I attended high school while there and received straight A's. I also played on the volleyball team and was awarded for my ability to play. Despite the positive outcome to treatment, when I was discharged, my parents did not allow me to return home. I think they were ashamed to call me their daughter and why shouldn't they be? I just returned home after being what society would call a prostitute. At that point, I began living at the St. Vincent De Paul, Toussaint Teen Center and started working a part-time job. After my eighteenth birthday, I ended up back in unhealthy relationships. One of these relationships would end up being an eleven year relationship that would take me through early adulthood as a victim of domestic violence.

This relationship would physically and mentally tear me down to a point of feelings of worthlessness and insignificance. My life throughout this relationship was spent making the other person happy, despite my own feelings. I felt as if I could not have any feelings and any I did develop, did not matter. He would tell me that I would never be anything, no one would ever want me, and if I did not want to do what he wanted me to, someone else would. So I tried to put more effort into pleasing him and never really felt valued or like I had a mind of my own. He would discredit the things I did do for him and say they weren't good enough. Though the relationship did not begin this way it developed into this. In the beginning, he appeared to want to take care of me and play the role of the provider and protector of the relationship. I had no idea that he could be so mean until the first time he shifted to a real life Dr. Jekyll and Mr. Hyde.

His mental abuse did not change over the course of the relationship, even with our active participation in Church. His physical violence would often follow his verbal attack, depending on my response. If I was submissive to his verbal attack and did not respond, he would continue verbally, however, if I did respond he would become physical. I can recall one day sitting down with the Pastor of the Church we attended and letting him know that I was being abused at which time he scheduled an appointment with the two of us. The Pastor's conclusion was that I pray harder for my husband and that God does not condone divorce. This was his statement even after I confided in him about the abuse and my abuser confirmed it.

As a follower of that Church, I did just as the Pastor suggested, however, things did not seem to change; they appeared to get worse. I even sought Church counseling to help me understand what I was possibly doing wrong. Half way through the counseling sessions, I was informed by the counselors that they had specific instructions from the Pastor to stop counseling me. I was in total disbelief and shock. I was left to figure out this situation on my own and after the shock settled, I began praying for God to help me understand if and why He would be okay with me being physically abused.

This led me to research to understand God's thoughts on abuse. I searched for books and attempted to find the answers I so yearned for. After weeks of looking and reading, I was finally pointed in the right direction; I believe by the Holy Spirit, because there was not one book that I could find that answered my questions. The Holy Spirit led me to God's word, The Holy Bible. As I began to read and study the more I began to understand that God is not okay with abuse. Anything other than love is contradictory of who God is and being abused is not an act of love. God is about love and nowhere in His word does it condone a man abusing a woman or vice versa. God clearly tells us what love is and is not and He shows us through the life of Jesus, how we are to express love.

If I give everything I own to the poor and even go to the stake to be burned as a martyr, but I do not love, I've gotten nowhere. So, no matter what I say, what I believe, and what I do, I'm bankrupt without love, Love never gives up, Love cares more for others than for self. Love doesn't strut, Doesn't have a swelled head. Doesn't force itself on others, Isn't always "me first," Doesn't fly off the handle, Doesn't keep score of the sins of others, Doesn't revel when others grovel, Takes pleasure in the flowering of truth, Puts up with anything, Trust God always, Always looks for the best, Never looks back, But keeps going to the end. (1 Corinthians 13:3-7 MSG)

I hung onto these words and began praying that God would reveal to me the heart of the man who was abusing me. I asked God to show me who this man really was. I had been promised numerous times that he would stop. He never really said what he would change; however, I hoped that he would stand by his words and strive to change his behavior. At times there were brief moments (days) that he was not abusive, however it was inevitable to return and the sad part is; I knew that and still stayed. I even began to fast as I yearned for God's revelation into this man. As the fast came to an end it was clear to me that this was not the relationship God had for me and no way could any Pastor or Church member tell me to stay in this situation and just pray harder for this man. God did show me who this man was as each day the violence escalated. At this time, I was certain that this relationship had to end. I had to leave no matter what I lost in the process, so I strategically left.

Leaving felt like the most difficult thing I had ever done because the image we portrayed to others was of a happy home, a somewhat happy marriage, and the "white picket fence." This would all be destroyed and I carried the guilt of being the reason for the destruction. This feeling is what often led to my decision to stay in the relationship. Furthermore, I knew that when I left, I would leave with nothing. He even told me that if I ever left him, I could not take anything, not even my children. He made it clear that I would be nothing without him and if I left him; he would kill me. I believed his threat to end my life as this was the same man that found me each time I had left him before. He went through some of the most terrifying depths to locate me. He drove through three states in a matter of nine hours to locate me. I knew what he was capable of and I knew if I was leaving it would require a strategic exit plan, so I thought. Well the plan did not go as I planned. I ended up nearly losing my life to him and had to live in a home where I had to cover up every window, change the locks on the all the doors, sleep in one room of the five bedroom house–with all my children. However I did eventually get away with my children and most of our belongings.

During the course of this relationship, I recall leaving with my children and sleeping in the car in the airport parking lot because there was not one shelter with space for us. As the intake person explained to me, funding had been cut and all the shelters were full. She then said try back tomorrow after 8:00a.m. I had nowhere to go until I had this thought that the hourly airport parking lot is a safe place because they have cameras and people are always coming and going. I drove 45 minutes to the airport and placed blankets in the windows and rolled them up to block out the lights so my children could sleep. I was awaked most of the night and early the next morning I called the shelters again. Unfortunately, they advised me to check into a hotel because they would not have any space and they could not help with the cost of the hotel room. I had no other choice but to check into a hotel and wait to call the list of shelters again at 4:00p.m. Again they had no space available. I knew that this was not fair to my children and I wanted nothing more than for them to be able to sleep in their own beds. At that moment, I had a decision to make, live on the streets with my children – in the car, or to go back to my abuser. During this particular time, I chose the latter.

CHAPTER 10

A NEW JOURNEY, A NEW LIFE

In his kindness God called you to share in his eternal glory by means of Christ Jesus. So after you have suffered for a little while, he will restore, support, and strengthen you, and he will place you on a firm foundation. (1 Peter 5:10 NLT)

I had attended college classes on and off since I was eighteen years old and had a plan of becoming a Registered Nurse. Shortly after leaving the abusive relationship, for the last time, I became more involved and proactive in my education. I had attended several prerequisite classes to fulfill my desire. One day, I received a letter from the University stating that if I did not receive straight A's for that particular semester; I would not be eligible for the RN program. I wasn't sure if I was capable of or could get straight A's. While in college, it seemed like no matter how hard I tried, I could not get straight A's. I could get all B's but not A's, no way. After receiving this letter I prayed. I wasn't sure what God wanted from me because I had worked hard and dedicated everything to getting into this program. My livelihood and my children's future depended on it.

This journey to become an RN initially began shortly after high school. I would randomly attend college and take one class at a time, hoping to reach the goal one day. So after receiving this letter and praying, I asked the Heavenly Father to tell me what He wanted me to do and to put me where He wanted me. I truly wanted nothing more than to be what His plan was for me. I was exhausted doing things my way as they seemed to take me nowhere. I then went to see my advisor. She asked me what I wanted to do. I had this generic response and said I wanted to help people. She then asked me if I had considered social work. I said no and insisted that I had no desire to take kids away from their parents. She smiled and said, "There is more to social work than that." She encouraged me to attend a class that would give me a broader understanding about the field of Social Work. Eventually I agreed to take the class and enjoyed it. This led me to consider applying for this program. There were two programs at the University that students had to apply to, one was nursing and the other was social work. I hesitated when it came to applying for fear that I would be denied, however, I kept feeling like God was leading me to apply. In the final hour of the submission deadline I applied for the social work program.

A few weeks passed and I did not put much thought into my acceptance because I did not expect it to happen. I actually expected to be denied due to the many other failures I had in my life. When I received a letter in the mail from the University, I eagerly opened it. At first I was hesitant. As I opened the letter I didn't even read it, I skimmed it. I noticed the word "Congratulations," which prompted me to read the letter entirely. It read, "Congratulations you have been accepted." I was ecstatic. At this moment, I knew that the Father had just put me where He wanted me to be and I began working toward a new degree in Social Work.

Shortly after beginning the program, I sat down with my social work advisor who informed me that I would not be eligible for the Honor Society that I had so desperately wanted to be a part of. According to my transcript, I did not have the required GPA and she did not foresee me achieving that GPA before graduation. When she said that, I recall looking at her and saying, "the God I serve says differently." During my second to last semester, I received a letter informing me that I would not have enough financial aid to complete my education requirements for graduation. I prayed and was lead to appeal the financial aid decision. I waited for the response to the appeal and it was granted and I was able to complete all the required classes not for just one bachelor's degree, but two.

A few weeks before graduation, I was informed that my GPA was a 3.00 and I could now become a member of the Honor Society. When I walked across the stage during graduation, my social work advisor was there to greet me and we both smiled at one another as I said to her, "we did it." A couple of months before graduating from my undergraduate studies I had began applying for graduate school. With encouragement from the Holy Spirit, I applied to five graduate schools. I was accepted at two universities; I turned down one, I was denied at one, and waitlisted at another. One of the schools I was accepted at had an accelerated Master's degree program that would require an intensive summer study, and a significant out of pocket expense.

Three months before graduating with my undergraduate degrees, my car was stolen from in front of my apartment. It was later revealed that the man who abused me for eleven years had come and taken the car in the middle of the night. This was another obstacle that I had to pray through as I knew that God had to have a plan because I know He did not get me that far to leave me. I had a friend from school who reached out to me after hearing about my car being taken. Her daughter had a car that she wasn't using and she asked me if I needed to borrow it until I could get another one. I was blown away by her kindness and I used her car to get to and from college and my internship. I had to drive an hour one way to and from school. This was nothing more than a blessing and an intervention from the Heavenly Father.

Just prior to attending graduate school, I received a sum of money. I just knew this money was to buy a car. I even felt that God had blessed me with the money just for that purpose. I had kids and I needed to get a car. I prayed and was led to hold onto the money for a couple of months. Prior to attending graduate school, I had to attend the orientation. During this orientation the instructor told us that we would have to pay our summer fee before starting the program. That evening I went home and applied for a loan to pay for the summer session and was denied. This led me to think that maybe I was making a mistake and that this was God's way of saying no to graduate school. I began to pray at that very moment and realized that the money I needed for the summer session was the exact amount of money that I had received in the mail.

This was a hard decision for me as I tried to figure out how I was going to buy a car and pay for school. I called my friend, who was lending me her car and told her the situation. She told me to use her car for a little while longer. The next day, I paid for graduate school and ten months later I graduated with a Master's degree. Though there was a gap of time where she needed her car back and having the ability to purchase one, God still made a way and I was in a rental car every week for about three months. Looking back at my finances there is no way that I could explain this and the amount of money I was receiving was not nearly enough to pay my rent. Prior to graduating with a Masters Degree, I had a job waiting. Not only was I able to graduate while being a single mom of four, by the grace of God, He made it possible for me to graduate with a 4.00 GPA. Now that is the magnificence of God and His power.

CONCLUSION

God has been faithful to who He is. He has never left me, even when I made decisions for my life; He never abandoned me. He shielded me and saved me. The greatest joy to me is that I know God loves me and it is not some superficial worldly view of love, but He really loves me. He took me, the most unworthy, insignificant, invaluable (to society), unimportant woman and made me worthy and He wants to do the same for EVERYONE. His design for our lives was never to be insufficient to the Earth. He always has had and always will have a plan and purpose for each of us.

In society's eyes, I was nothing except for garbage and if I had died I'm not sure too many people would have noticed. I was seen as a woman who probably should be addicted to drugs, selling my body, being unproductive, uneducated, incarcerated, or dead. I am a single mom of five, all of which went through portions of this journey with me. I managed to do the unthinkable and unlikely because I asked God to transform, restore, renew, and heal me. This process took faith, trust, forgiveness, and determination. God's plans for me were greater and better than any plan I ever had for myself. I surrendered my life to Him because I had been tired of feeling insignificant. I wanted my children to have a life better than than the one I had growing up and I knew it would take a huge change in what I had been doing and the help of the Heavenly Father.

I yearned for what God had to offer because I spent a significant portion of my life doing what I thought was best and that did not get me positive results. I knew and believed that He could make me new and He can do the same for you. His promises are true and will never return void. His desire is to have a relationship with each one of us and to give us the BEST life that we could ever imagine as we trust in Him, His will, and have faith that He is going to do what He says He will do. The Bible is full of His promises and He will do what He promises.

Though my life has had many challenges, God took the time to hear my prayers, my cries and carry me through the toughest times of my life. Being determined to be different and to strive through tough times is not easy, that I know, but God can help us make those times not so difficult. Since I have made the obedient decision to share my story with others and surrender my life to God, He has continued to remain faithful in His promises. He has continued to bless me and my children and for that I am tremendously thankful and grateful. Please do not mistake what I say when I say God made me new. I still have daily challenges; the difference now is that I

Conclusion

know that I can call on Him to help me get through any challenges. He helps me see the lessons I need to learn, and He holds me in times when I may feel weak, lonely, or find myself struggling. I have found that doing things His way is less stressful and will result in a positive outcome even if initially it appears challenging.

I now look at situations in a different manner and when in doubt, I evaluate the situation to see how it can be of benefit to my life. When something is from God it will not be harmful to us. He has helped to change the way I think and how I see things and He can do the same for you. I used to see myself as the world saw me, now I see myself as God sees me. No longer does my past dictate my future. No longer do I believe that because I sin; I must continue sinning. The bondage of sin does not get to anchor me or control my life any longer. God's salvation is available to everyone and at any time we can ask Him to forgive us, build a relationship with Him at the same time we learn to change our ways. God has given us freewill to walk away, ask to be forgiven, change our ways, and know that we are His precious creation. Jesus was sacrificed for our sins so we no longer have to live in condemnation and He loves us more than our minds could ever imagine.

I am flawless.
I am valuable.
I am made in His image.
I am His precious creation.
I am uniquely created by my Heavenly Father's own hands.
I am created with a plan and purpose.
I am valued.
I am treasured.
I am beautiful.
I am cherished.
I am loved.
I am a gift
and so are you!

When you are feeling weak and weary, remember who God created you to be and how His promises are made just for you!

ACKNOWLEDGMENTS

I will forever be grateful to the Heavenly Father who took me, molded me, and shaped me into the creation He always believed me to be. I graciously thank my children for going through this journey with me and their patience through each step. I am thankful for those individuals I have met along the way. I appreciate, with a full heart, those individuals who heard my testimony and allowed me the setting to share it and positively impact the lives of others. I am appreciative to each professor, advisor, and counselor who believed in me and to those who prayed over me and for me even when I did not know it. My heart is full as I think about those who may have played a small role, in their eyes, yet it was huge in the overall picture. God took the time to care about every aspect of this journey from the beginning of my life up to now and as I look at His magnificence, being thankful does not seem like enough. I am glad that He sees me and sees the gratitude within me. I am thankful for the future that becomes brighter and brighter each day. Our God is truly an AWESOME God.

GOD'S PROMISES

"For I know the plans I have for you," says the Lord. "They are plans for good and not disaster, to give you a future and a hope. In those days when you pray, I will listen. If you look for me wholeheartedly, you will find me.
(Jeremiah 29:11 NLT)

In his kindness God called you to share in his eternal glory by means of Christ Jesus. So after you have suffered for a little while, he will restore, support, and strengthen you, and he will place you on a firm foundation.
(1 Peter 5:10 NLT)

Don't be afraid, for I am with you. Don't be discouraged, for I am your God. I will strengthen you up with my victorious right hand.
(Isaiah 41:10 NLT)

But those who trust in the Lord will find new strength. They will soar high on wings like eagles. They will run and not grow weary. They will walk and not faint.
(Isaiah 40:31 NLT)

Even when I walk through the darkest valley, I will not be afraid, for you are close beside me. Your rod and your staff comfort me.
(Psalm 23:4 NLT)

And we know that God causes everything to work together for the good of those who love God and are called according to his purpose for them.
(Romans 8:28 NLT)

For I can do everything through Christ, who gives me strength.
(Philippians 4:13 NLT)

Let us come boldly to the throne of our gracious God. There we will receive his mercy, and we will find grace to help us when we need it most.
(Hebrews 4:16 NLT)

Don't worry about anything instead, pray about everything. Tell God what you need, and thank him for all he has done. Then you will experience God's peace, which exceeds anything we can understand. His peace will guard your hearts and minds as you live in Christ Jesus.
(Philippians 4:6-7 NLT)

Open your mouth and taste, open your eyes and see— how good God is. Blessed are you who run to him. Worship God if you want the best; worship opens doors to all his goodness.
(Psalm 34:8-9 MSG)

~ These are some of God's promises that are found in the Bible. ~
~ Please see the Bible for more promises of hope, love, restoration, healing, and much more! ~

~ ENDNOTES ~

To contact the author write:
Kelly Cody
900 East Fayette Street
Box 23021
Baltimore, Maryland 21203
or call (951) 977-1388

Email: myluv4god@hotmail.com
prov31ntrng@gmail.com

Twitter: @PROV31nTRNG
Facebook: www.facebook.com/PROVERBS31nTRAINING

Prayer requests are welcome.
Any communication, testimonies or help this book has provided are welcomed and greatly appreciated.

www.ingramcontent.com/pod-product-compliance
Ingram Content Group UK Ltd.
Pitfield, Milton Keynes, MK11 3LW, UK
UKHW041944230426
12048UKWH00008B/121